Alaska
Travel Guide 2025/2026

Explore the Last Frontier: Insider Tips and Expert Advice

Julie Z. Leftwich

All Rights Reserved

No part of this publication may be reproduced, distributed, or transmitted in any form or by any means, including photocopying, recording, or other electronic or mechanical methods, without the prior written permission of the publisher, except in the case of brief quotations embodied in critical reviews and certain other non-commercial uses permitted by copyright law.

Copyright © 2025 by Julie Z. Leftwich

Disclaimer

This travel guide is provided for informational purposes only. The information contained herein is believed to be accurate and reliable as of the publication date, but may be subject to change. We are not making any warranty, express or implied, with respect to the content of this guide.

Users of this guide are responsible for verifying information independently and consulting appropriate authorities and resources prior to travel. We are not liable for any loss or damage caused by the reliance on information contained in this guide.

Information regarding travel advisories, visas, health, safety, and other important considerations can change rapidly. Users are advised to check for the most up-to-date information from official government and travel industry sources before embarking on any trip.

Travel inherently involves risk, and users are responsible for making their own informed decisions and accepting any associated risks.

Table of Contents

Chapter 1: 7

Introduction to Alaska Cruises 7

   Overview of Alaska as a Cruise Destination 7

   Why Choose an Alaska Cruise in 2025/2026 9

   Map of Alaska 12

Chapter 2: Planning Your Alaska Cruise 13

   Choosing the Right Cruise Line 13

   Best Times to Cruise Alaska 15

   Itineraries and Ports of Call 18

Chapter 3: Cruise Preparation 21

   Packing Essentials for Alaska 21

   Travel Documentation and Requirements 23

   Health and Safety Considerations 25

   Map of Things to do in Alaska 28

Chapter 4: Onboard Experience 29

   Accommodations: Luxury vs. Affordable Options 29

   Dining Experiences: Top Restaurants on Board 31

   Activities and Entertainment 34

Chapter 5: Shore Excursions 37

    Popular Shore Excursions 37

    Unique Experiences: Wildlife and Nature Tours 39

    Family-Friendly Activities 41

    Map of Beaches in Alaska 44

Chapter 6: Wildlife Encounters 45

    Key Wildlife Species to Expect 45

    Responsible Wildlife Viewing Practices 47

    Best Locations for Wildlife Spotting 49

Chapter 7: Post-Cruise Options 51

    Exploring Alaska After Your Cruise 51

    Recommended Tours and Activities 53

    Travel Tips for Extended Stays 55

    Map of Hiking Trails in Alaska 58

Chapter 8: Booking Your Cruise 59

    How to Book Your Alaska Cruise 59

    Contact Information for Major Cruise Lines 61

    Tips for Getting the Best Deals 63

Chapter 9: Conclusion 66

    Recap of Key Points 66

Final Tips for an Unforgettable Alaska Cruise.............. 68

BONUS 71

    TRAVEL PLANNER.. 71

    TRAVEL BUDGET PLANNER 73

    NOTEPAD 74

Chapter 1: Introduction to Alaska Cruises

Overview of Alaska as a Cruise Destination

Alaska, often referred to as the Last Frontier, has emerged as an unparalleled cruise destination, captivating travelers with its stunning landscapes, rich culture, and abundant wildlife. The state's coastline stretches over 6,640 miles, offering an array of breathtaking vistas that range from towering glaciers to lush forests. Each port of call reveals a unique aspect of Alaskan life, ensuring that every journey is filled with discovery. Travelers can expect to encounter not only the natural beauty of the region but also the warm hospitality of its communities, making for a truly memorable cruise experience.

For families, couples, and solo travelers alike, Alaska cruises provide a variety of activities and excursions to cater to all interests. From wildlife watching in Glacier Bay National Park to dog sledding on a glacier, the adventure options are limitless. Families can enjoy educational programs about marine life, while couples might prefer romantic sunset cruises or intimate dining experiences featuring local cuisine.

Luxury accommodations are available onboard most cruise lines, offering a high level of service and comfort, while affordable options ensure that all travelers can enjoy the wonders of Alaska without breaking the bank.

Dining in Alaska is a highlight of any cruise, with a focus on fresh seafood and locally sourced ingredients. Onboard restaurants often feature menus that celebrate Alaska's culinary heritage, including dishes such as salmon, halibut, and king crab. Port towns offer additional opportunities to explore local eateries, ranging from casual fish shacks to upscale dining experiences. Notable restaurants like The Crow's Nest in Anchorage and the Fresh Catch Café in Ketchikan are highly recommended for their exceptional food and stunning views. Reservations are advisable, especially during peak cruise season.

As you plan your Alaska cruise for 2025/2026, it's essential to consider the various itineraries available. Popular

routes often include stops in Juneau, Skagway, and Sitka, each providing unique experiences and attractions. Booking a cruise well in advance is advisable to secure the best rates and desired cabin selections. For assistance with bookings, cruise lines typically provide dedicated customer service lines, making it easy to find the right cruise for your needs. Additionally, travel agents specializing in Alaskan cruises can offer invaluable insights and personalized recommendations.

Wildlife enthusiasts will find Alaska to be a paradise, with opportunities to see bears, whales, eagles, and more in their natural habitats. Many excursions are available that focus specifically on wildlife viewing, such as whale watching tours or guided hikes through national parks. These experiences not only allow for incredible photo opportunities but also offer a deeper understanding of Alaska's unique ecosystem. Whether you seek adventure or relaxation, an Alaska cruise promises to deliver an unforgettable journey through one of the most spectacular regions of the world.

Why Choose an Alaska Cruise in 2025/2026

Choosing an Alaska cruise in 2025/2026 presents an unparalleled opportunity to immerse yourself in the breathtaking beauty and vibrant culture of the Last Frontier. With advancements in cruise itineraries and offerings, travelers can now experience a perfect blend of adventure and relaxation, tailored to suit families, couples, and

solo adventurers alike. The stunning landscapes, from majestic glaciers to lush forests, provide a backdrop for a journey unlike any other, ensuring memories that last a lifetime.

Alaska's cruise season is set to be particularly vibrant in 2025 and 2026, with an array of itineraries that cater to various interests and budgets. Families can take advantage of kid-friendly programs and accommodations, while couples may indulge in romantic excursions and ne dining options on board. For those seeking luxury, premium cruise lines are introducing high-end amenities and personalized services, ensuring that every facet of the journey is extraordinary. Conversely, affordable options are available, making this remarkable experience accessible to all.

Wildlife enthusiasts will find that an Alaska cruise offers unrivaled opportunities to witness the region's diverse fauna. From whale watching excursions to guided tours in national parks, the wildlife encounters are numerous and unforgettable. The chance to see orcas, sea lions, and brown bears in their natural habitat elevates the cruise experience into a captivating adventure. This immersive wildlife exploration is complemented by onboard presentations from naturalists, providing valuable insights into the ecosystems you will encounter.

Dining aboard an Alaska cruise is an adventure in itself. The region is known for its fresh seafood, and many cruise lines pride themselves on serving locally sourced ingredients in their restaurants. Whether you prefer casual dining with family or an upscale meal with a view, there are options to satisfy every palate. Notable restaurants, such as the Alaska Fish House and the Glacier Bay Lodge Dining Room, offer unique culinary experiences that can be enjoyed before or after your cruise, enhancing your overall journey.

Booking your Alaska cruise for 2025/2026 is straightforward, with numerous resources available to help you plan the perfect getaway. Contact a travel agent specializing in cruises or reach out directly to cruise lines like Princess Cruises at 1-800-774-6237 or Holland America Line at 1-877-932-4259 for personalized assistance. With the right planning, you can secure the best accommodations and excursions, ensuring your Alaska cruise adventure is both enjoyable and stress-free. Embrace the opportunity to explore Alaska's stunning landscapes, rich wildlife, and exquisite dining options, making this journey one you and your loved ones will cherish forever.

Map of Alaska

https://maps.app.goo.gl/v1ZzSkNpP7wZqaNn9

SCAN IMAGE /QR CODE WITH YOUR PHONE TO GET THE LOCATION IN REAL TIME

Chapter 2: Planning Your Alaska Cruise

Choosing the Right Cruise Line

Choosing the right cruise line for your Alaskan adventure is essential to ensuring an unforgettable experience. With various options available, including luxury liners, family-friendly vessels, and budget-conscious choices, it is vital to assess your priorities and preferences before making a decision. Factors such as onboard amenities, dining options, excursion offerings, and overall atmosphere should be taken into account to match your expectations with the cruise line's features. Additionally, consider the cruise line's reputation for customer service and passenger satisfaction, which can significantly influence your overall enjoyment.

For families, choosing a cruise line that caters to children and offers family-oriented activities is crucial. Lines like Disney Cruise Line and Royal Caribbean are known for their exceptional family programs, including kids' clubs, family dining options, and engaging entertainment. These cruise lines provide a blend of adventure and relaxation, making it easier for parents to enjoy their vacation while keeping the children entertained. On the other hand, couples seeking a romantic getaway may prefer cruise lines such as Princess Cruises or Holland America Line, which often focus on intimate dining experiences, serene spa options, and scenic balcony accommodations.

Luxury travelers seeking an elevated experience should explore cruise lines like Seabourn and Silversea. These lines offer all-inclusive packages, featuring gourmet dining, personalized shore excursions, and exclusive onboard activities. The service provided on luxury cruises is often unparalleled, with a higher staff-to-guest ratio ensuring personalized attention throughout your journey. If your budget allows for a more lavish experience, consider these options, as they can create lasting memories while exploring the breathtaking landscapes of Alaska.

For travelers looking for affordable accommodation without sacrificing quality, lines such as Carnival Cruise Line and Norwegian Cruise Line present excellent value. These cruise lines often provide a range of cabin options that cater to different budgets, along with diverse dining venues and entertainment choices. While some amenities may be more basic than  their luxury counterparts, the overall experience can still be delightful, especially when considering the stunning Alaskan scenery and vibrant ports of call. Prioritizing what aspects are most important to your travel group will help in narrowing down the best choice.

Finally, to book your cruise, it is advisable to contact the cruise lines directly or consult a travel agent specializing in Alaska cruise travel. Popular cruise lines can be reached through their customer service hotlines, and many have dedicated sections on their websites for inquiries and reservations. Top restaurants on board can vary by cruise line, but many offer exceptional dining experiences featuring fresh, local ingredients, allowing you to savor the f l avors of Alaska as you cruise. Taking the time to thoroughly research and compare cruise lines will ultimately lead to a well-planned and memorable Alaskan cruise adventure.

Best Times to Cruise Alaska

When considering the best times to cruise Alaska, it is crucial to understand the seasonal variations that can significantly enhance your experience. The peak cruising season in Alaska runs from late May to mid-September. This period offers the most favorable weather conditions, with temperatures typically ranging from the mid-50s to mid-70s Fahrenheit. During these months, the days are long, allowing for ample daylight to enjoy the stunning landscapes and abundant wildlife. Families, couples, and individuals seeking luxury or affordable accommodations will find that this time frame presents the best opportunities for excursions and activities, including glacier tours, wildlife sightings, and cultural experiences.

June is particularly appealing for travelers who wish to experience Alaska at its most vibrant. The flora is in full bloom, and wildlife is actively visible, making it an ideal time for nature enthusiasts. This month is also popular among families, as schools are out, and various shore excursions are available to cater to all ages. For those considering luxury cruises, many premium lines offer special amenities and activities in June, enhancing the onboard experience. Booking during this month can provide access to exclusive deals and promotions that may not be available later in the season.

July is another prime month for cruising Alaska, marked by warmer temperatures and an abundance of wildlife. This time is especially favorable for viewing humpback whales, sea lions, and other marine life, enticing couples and families alike. Many cruise lines schedule additional shore excursions during this time, including fishing trips and kayaking adventures, allowing passengers to immerse themselves in the stunning Alaskan landscape. July is also when several local festivals occur, providing a unique cultural experience for those looking to explore beyond the natural beauty.

August marks the transition from summer to fall, and while temperatures may start to cool, this month still offers excellent cruising conditions. The crowds begin to thin out, making it a more peaceful experience for those seeking a quieter adventure. Wildlife sightings remain plentiful, as bears and moose are often spotted preparing for winter. For travelers interested in luxury accommodations, many cruise lines offer discounts and packages during this shoulder season, making it an attractive option for those who want a premium experience without the peak-season prices.

Finally, September presents a unique opportunity for travelers looking to experience the early autumn beauty of Alaska. The foliage begins to change, creating a breathtaking backdrop for cruising. Although the weather can be more unpredictable, the fewer crowds mean a more intimate experience with nature and local culture. Many cruise lines offer special itineraries and themed cruises during this month, catering to various interests, from photography to culinary

experiences. For those seeking a balance between adventure and relaxation, September is an excellent time to explore Alaska's majestic landscapes while enjoying luxurious amenities and top-notch dining options onboard.

Itineraries and Ports of Call

Itineraries and ports of call play a crucial role in shaping the experience of an Alaska cruise. In 2025 and 2026, travelers can expect a variety of itineraries that cater to diverse interests, whether you are a family seeking adventure, a couple looking for romance, or travelers interested in luxurious or budget-friendly accommodations. Different cruise lines offer distinct routes, which may include popular destinations such as Juneau, Ketchikan, and Skagway, each with its unique charm and activities. It's essential to choose an itinerary that aligns with your interests, ensuring memorable experiences in the breathtaking Alaskan wilderness.

Juneau, the state capital, is renowned for its stunning landscapes and rich history. Here, visitors can explore the Mendenhall Glacier, take a guided tour to learn about the region's indigenous culture, or indulge in fresh seafood at top-rated restaurants like Tracy's King Crab Shack. Families can enjoy activities such as whale watching or visiting the Alaska State Museum, while couples might prefer a romantic stroll through the picturesque downtown. With its combination of adventure and relaxation, Juneau serves as an ideal port of call on any Alaskan itinerary.

Ketchikan, often referred to as the "Salmon Capital of the World," offers a unique blend of natural beauty and cultural experiences. The vibrant arts scene, highlighted by totem poles and local galleries, provides an enriching experience for all ages. Families can participate in fi shing excursions or explore the nearby Misty Fjords National Monument, while couples may find delight in the scenic views and quaint charm of Creek Street. Dining options abound, with local favorites such as The Alaska Fish House and The Landing offering delicious meals that showcase the region's seafood bounty.

Skagway presents a historical narrative intertwined with stunning landscapes and outdoor activities. Known for its Gold Rush history, visitors can explore the Klondike Gold Rush National Historical Park or take a scenic ride on the White Pass & Yukon Route Railroad. Skagway's charming downtown features numerous shops and eateries, making it an excellent stop for families looking to soak in local culture or couples seeking a picturesque setting for a romantic getaway. No visit would be complete without savoring the local cuisine at places like Red Onion Saloon, where the history and f l avor of Alaska come together.

As you plan your Alaska cruise adventure, consider the itineraries and ports of call that best suit your interests and preferences. Each port offers unique opportunities for exploration, dining, and connection with the stunning landscapes of Alaska. Make sure to book your excursions in advance and check with your cruise line for recommendations on accommodations and dining. For further assistance, you can contact cruise line representatives or local tour operators to gain insights into the best options for your travel needs. Enjoy your journey through one of the world's most magnificent regions, where every port of call promises a new adventure waiting to unfold.

Chapter 3: Cruise Preparation

Packing Essentials for Alaska

When preparing for an Alaskan cruise, packing the right essentials can significantly enhance your experience. The unique weather conditions and diverse activities available in Alaska necessitate careful consideration of your wardrobe and gear. Layering is key; consider packing moisture-wicking base layers, insulating mid-layers, and a waterproof outer layer to keep you warm and dry. A lightweight, insulated jacket is particularly beneficial for the chilly evenings and unexpected weather changes. Additionally, a wide-brimmed hat and sunglasses are essential for protecting yourself from the sun's glare, especially when reflected off glaciers and water.

Footwear should not be

overlooked, as you'll likely engage in activities ranging from hiking to exploring charming port towns. Waterproof hiking boots with good traction are ideal for excursions, while comfortable shoes or sandals are perfect for relaxing on the ship. Don't forget to pack a pair of warm socks to keep your feet cozy during cooler days. For those who prefer luxury, consider investing in high-quality outdoor gear that combines style with functionality, ensuring you look great while staying comfortable.

Accessories can make a significant difference in your overall enjoyment. A reliable pair of binoculars is invaluable for wildlife watching, allowing you to spot whales, eagles, and other magnificent creatures from a distance. A compact backpack is practical for day trips, providing space for essentials like water bottles, snacks, and a camera. Additionally, a portable charger for your devices will help ensure you capture every moment without worrying about battery life during excursions.

When it comes to personal items, consider your skincare and health needs. The crisp Alaskan air can be drying, so packing a good moisturizer and lip balm is advisable. If you take any medications, ensure you have enough for the duration of your trip, along with a small first-aid kit that includes band-aids, pain relievers, and any necessary prescriptions. It's also wise to bring insect repellent as the warmer months can attract mosquitoes, particularly in more forested areas.

Lastly, do not forget to include travel documents and essentials such as your cruise tickets, identification, and insurance information. Keeping these items in a waterproof pouch will protect them during your adventures. For those seeking recommendations on local dining, consider researching top restaurants at each port of call. Many cruise lines provide resources for booking excursions and dining, so be sure to utilize those services to enhance your Alaskan cruise experience. With thoughtful packing and preparation, you can focus on enjoying the breathtaking beauty and rich experiences Alaska has to offer.

Travel Documentation and Requirements

Travel documentation is a critical aspect of planning your Alaskan cruise adventure. Passengers must ensure they possess the proper identification and paperwork to board their cruise ship and explore the enchanting landscapes of Alaska. For U.S. citizens, a valid passport is essential for international travel, especially if your cruise itinerary includes destinations in Canada. While some travelers may consider using a passport card, it is not accepted for air travel or for cruises that dock at foreign ports. Therefore, it is advisable to secure a full passport to avoid any complications during your journey.

In addition to passports, travelers should be aware of any specific

requirements related to their cruise line. Many cruise lines enforce their own documentation policies, which may include additional identification or health forms, particularly in light of recent health and safety protocols. It is prudent to check with your cruise line well ahead of your departure date to ensure you have all necessary documents. This proactive approach helps to minimize stress and ensures a smoother embarkation process.

Travelers should also consider any visa requirements based on their nationality. While most visitors from countries that participate in the Visa Waiver Program do not need a visa for short visits, it's essential to verify your specific situation before making travel arrangements. Additionally, families traveling with minors should carry extra documentation, such as birth certificates, to verify age and parental consent if only one parent is traveling with the child. Ensuring all family members have the correct documentation can save time and prevent potential issues at the port.

Health documentation is another important consideration for those embarking on a cruise to Alaska. Depending on your cruise line,

you may be required to provide proof of vaccinations or complete health questionnaires. As health regulations can frequently change, it is vital to stay informed about current requirements related to vaccinations and health precautions. Carrying a copy of your vaccination records can expedite boarding and ensure compliance with any health and safety protocols aboard the ship.

Finally, it is advisable to keep copies of all travel documents, including your passport, cruise itinerary, and any health-related paperwork. Storing these copies securely and having them accessible can be invaluable if the originals are lost or stolen. Consider using a travel app or cloud storage service to keep digital copies as a backup. With proper preparation and organization, you can focus on enjoying the breathtaking vistas and unique experiences that Alaska has to offer.

Health and Safety Considerations

Health and safety considerations are paramount when planning an Alaska cruise adventure, as the unique environment and remote locations present specific challenges. Travelers should be aware of the varying weather conditions that can change rapidly, requiring appropriate clothing and gear. Layering is essential, as temperatures can fluctuate throughout the day.

Waterproof and windproof jackets, sturdy footwear, and sun protection are necessary to ensure comfort while engaging in outdoor activities like hiking or wildlife viewing. It is advisable to check weather forecasts regularly and prepare for unexpected changes.

In addition to weather preparedness, health precautions should be taken into account. Travelers should consult with their healthcare providers regarding vaccinations and medications, particularly for those with pre-existing health conditions. Sea sickness is another common concern; thus, individuals prone to motion sickness should consider preventative measures such as over-the-counter medications or acupressure bands. Staying hydrated and maintaining a balanced diet during the cruise are also vital to keeping energy levels up while exploring Alaska's stunning landscapes.

The remote nature of many Alaskan ports means that access to medical facilities can be limited. Passengers are encouraged to familiarize themselves with the medical services available on board their cruise ships. Most vessels are equipped with medical staff and facilities to handle minor injuries and illnesses. Travelers should also consider carrying a small first aid kit, including essentials such as pain relievers, antiseptic wipes, and any personal medications, to manage minor health issues that may arise during the trip.

Safety protocols extend beyond

personal health to include general safety measures while on excursions. Passengers should always follow the guidance of tour operators and crew members during excursions, especially when participating in activities such as kayaking, hiking, or wildlife viewing. It is essential to remain within designated areas, respect wildlife, and adhere to safety instructions provided by guides to ensure a safe and enjoyable experience. Additionally, travelers should familiarize themselves with the emergency procedures of the cruise line before embarking on their journey.

Finally, the importance of travel insurance cannot be overstated. Comprehensive travel insurance that covers health-related incidents, trip cancellations, and lost luggage can provide peace of mind during an Alaskan cruise. Travelers should assess their insurance options carefully and ensure they are adequately covered for the unique risks associated with cruising in Alaska. By prioritizing health and safety considerations, travelers can enjoy their Alaskan adventure with confidence, making the most of the breathtaking scenery and unforgettable experiences that await.

Map of Things to do in Alaska

https://maps.app.goo.gl/tZQCm9FDgN2wXVpVA

Chapter 4: Onboard Experience

Accommodations: Luxury vs. Affordable Options

Accommodations during your Alaska cruise can significantly influence your overall experience, as the choices range from luxurious to budget-friendly options. For travelers seeking a lavish experience, many cruise lines offer upscale suites equipped with private balconies, spacious living areas, and exclusive access to premium amenities. For instance, The Haven by Norwegian Cruise Line provides a private enclave with personal concierge service, ne dining, and a serene atmosphere. These luxurious choices often include complimentary excursions, gourmet dining options, and priority boarding, ensuring that every aspect of your cruise is tailored to provide an exceptional experience.

On the other hand, affordable accommodations are readily available and can still offer a comfortable and enjoyable stay without breaking the bank. Many cruise lines provide well-appointed cabins that cater to families and couples alike, designed with cozy furnishings and essential amenities. For example, Carnival Cruise Line features family-friendly cabins that maximize space and comfort, making them ideal for those traveling with children. Additionally, budget-conscious travelers can explore options like interior cabins or ocean-view staterooms, which allow guests to enjoy their cruise experience while keeping costs manageable.

When considering your budget, it is essential to factor in additional costs such as excursions, dining, and onboard activities. However, many cruise lines provide package deals that include shore excursions and meal plans, making it easier for families and couples to enjoy their time without overspending. For instance, Royal Caribbean offers bundled packages that combine dining and shore

excursions, allowing travelers to enjoy top attractions at a discounted rate. This approach ensures that guests can indulge in the beauty of Alaska while adhering to their financial plans.

Dining options on cruises can also vary significantly based on your accommodation choice. Luxury accommodations often grant access to exclusive restaurants featuring gourmet cuisine crafted by renowned chefs. For example, celebrity chef restaurants on select cruise lines offer a unique dining experience that showcases local Alaskan ingredients. In contrast, affordable dining venues provide a variety of options, from casual buffets to themed dining nights that cater to diverse tastes. Regardless of your accommodation choice, you can expect to sample a range of delectable dishes, including fresh seafood, hearty comfort foods, and international cuisine.

Ultimately, the choice between luxury and affordable accommodations will depend on your personal preferences and budget. Families seeking value may find that balanced options provide comfort without compromising the quality of their experience. Couples looking for a romantic getaway may prefer the indulgence of upscale accommodations that offer intimate settings and exclusive amenities. Regardless of your choice, Alaska's natural beauty and diverse activities will ensure a memorable cruise adventure, making it essential to select accommodations that align with your travel goals. For bookings, consider contacting major cruise lines directly or utilizing travel agencies specializing in Alaska cruises to secure the best deals and accommodations that suit your needs.

Dining Experiences: Top Restaurants on Board

Aboard Alaska cruise ships, dining transforms into a captivating experience that complements the stunning scenery outside. Guests can expect a variety of culinary options that reflect both local

f l avors and international cuisine. From casual eateries to upscale dining rooms, each restaurant offers a unique ambiance and menu that caters to diverse tastes. Families, couples, and solo travelers alike will find that the dining experiences available on these cruises are designed to create lasting memories while enjoying the breathtaking Alaskan backdrop.

One of the standout dining options is the signature restaurant, often featuring gourmet dishes inspired by the rich ingredients found in Alaskan waters and landscapes. Expect to savor fresh seafood, locally sourced meats, and seasonal vegetables, all prepared by talented chefs. Reservations are highly recommended, especially for popular dining times. For those interested in a more intimate dining experience, many cruise lines offer specialty restaurants with limited seating, providing an exclusive atmosphere perfect for couples looking to celebrate a special occasion.

For families aboard the cruise, casual dining venues are abundant, offering a wide range of choices that cater to even the pickiest of eaters. Buffet-style restaurants provide f l exibility, allowing guests to sample various dishes at their own pace. Kid-friendly menus ensure that younger travelers enjoy meals designed just for them. Additionally, themed dining nights can add excitement to the culinary journey, with options ranging from Italian to Mexican fare, making every meal an adventure.

Luxury options are also present for those seeking a more refined dining experience. Many cruise lines offer chef's tables or wine pairing dinners, where guests can indulge in multi-course meals complemented by carefully selected wines. These experiences often include interactions with the chefs, providing insight into the culinary process and the inspiration behind each dish. For those wishing to celebrate an anniversary or milestone, these upscale dining options provide an unforgettable way to mark the occasion amidst the splendor of the Alaskan wilderness.

To make reservations for these dining experiences, guests can contact the cruise line's customer service prior to boarding or utilize onboard concierge services once they are on the ship. Popular lines like Princess Cruises (1-800-774-6237) and Holland America Line (1-877-932-4259) offer easy access to reservation systems. By planning ahead, travelers can ensure they enjoy the best dining experiences

available on their Alaska cruise, making the journey not just a voyage of scenic beauty, but also a memorable culinary exploration.

Activities and Entertainment

When embarking on an Alaska cruise, the range of activities and entertainment options available is truly remarkable. From breathtaking natural scenery to vibrant cultural experiences, every moment onboard and ashore is designed to immerse travelers in the unique charm of the Last Frontier.
Families, couples, and solo adventurers alike will find an array of engaging pursuits that cater to their interests and preferences, ensuring each day is f i lled with excitement and discovery.

Onboard, cruise lines offer a plethora of entertainment options. Guests can enjoy live performances, including musical shows, comedy acts, and cultural presentations that showcase the rich heritage of Alaska. Many ships feature state-of-the-art theaters and lounges, providing comfortable venues for these events. Additionally, themed nights and trivia contests are popular among guests looking to connect with fellow travelers. For those seeking relaxation, spas and wellness programs offer a chance to unwind, while onboard pools and fitness centers keep travelers active throughout their journey.

Shore excursions are a highlight of any Alaska cruise, offering opportunities to explore the stunning landscapes and wildlife of the region. Adventure-seekers can partake in activities such as kayaking through serene fjords, hiking on scenic trails, or even dog sledding on glaciers. Families will appreciate family-friendly excursions that include wildlife viewing tours, where they can see bears, whales, and sea otters in their natural habitats. Each port of call, from Juneau to Ketchikan, boasts unique excursions that provide a taste of local culture and history, making it easy to tailor the experience to individual interests.

Dining is another essential aspect of the Alaskan cruise experience. Many cruise lines pride themselves on offering a diverse array of culinary options, featuring fresh, locally sourced seafood and regional specialties. Top restaurants onboard often include elegant dining rooms as well as casual eateries, ensuring that every palate is catered to. For those looking for a more luxurious experience, specialty dining venues offer gourmet meals paired with exquisite wines. Additionally, shore excursions often include visits to local eateries, allowing travelers to savor authentic Alaskan cuisine and immerse themselves in the local culture.

In summary, the activities and entertainment options available on an Alaska cruise are designed to create unforgettable memories. Whether guests prefer thrilling adventures, captivating performances, or delightful dining experiences, there is something for everyone to enjoy. By exploring both onboard and ashore, travelers can fully embrace the beauty and wonder of Alaska, ensuring their journey is one filled with joy and exploration. For those ready to book their adventure, contacting cruise lines directly will provide the latest offerings and availability for the 2025/2026 season.

Chapter 5: Shore Excursions

Popular Shore Excursions

When cruising through Alaska, shore excursions serve as the gateway to experiencing the region's breathtaking landscapes and vibrant culture. Popular shore excursions often include activities that appeal to a wide range of interests, making them suitable for families, couples, and travelers seeking both luxury and affordability. Whether you are looking to immerse yourself in the natural beauty of Alaska or explore its rich history, there is an excursion tailored just for you.

One of the most sought-after excursions is the Glacier Bay National Park tour. This majestic park is renowned for its stunning glaciers and diverse wildlife. Visitors can witness calving glaciers and spot seals, otters, and even humpback whales. Guided boat tours provide an intimate view of the glacial landscapes, and many operators offer lunch options featuring local seafood. Companies like Alaskan Dream Cruises can be reached at 1-877-747-8100 for booking inquiries and additional details.

Another popular choice is the dog sledding adventure, which showcases one of Alaska's most iconic experiences. Participants can take a scenic helicopter ride to a glacier, where they will meet a team of sled dogs and learn about their training and care. This excursion is particularly appealing for families and animal lovers, providing an unforgettable opportunity to engage with these remarkable dogs. Booking can be done through companies like Coastal Helicopters at 1-800-655-3220.

Those seeking a more cultural experience might consider visiting the historic town of Skagway. Here, travelers can explore the Klondike Gold Rush National Historical Park, where they can learn about the gold rush and its impact on the region. Guided walking tours lead visitors through the restored buildings and share stories of the prospectors who sought their fortunes. Local eateries, such as the Red Onion Saloon, offer hearty meals and a taste of the area's history, making it a perfect stop after your tour.

Finally, a whale watching excursion is a must for anyone looking to witness Alaska's marine life up close. These tours typically depart from major ports like Juneau and Sitka, taking you to prime locations where you can see humpback whales, orcas, and other marine species in their natural habitat. Many companies, including Harv and Marv's Outback Alaska, offer personalized experiences and can be reached at 1-907- 789-0700. With a variety of options available, you can tailor your excursions to create unforgettable memories in the stunning Alaskan wilderness.

Unique Experiences: Wildlife and Nature Tours

Alaska's wildlife and natural beauty create a unique backdrop for unforgettable experiences during your cruise adventure. From the moment you set sail, the allure of pristine landscapes and diverse ecosystems will captivate your senses. The opportunity to witness majestic creatures in their natural habitats, such as whales breaching the surface, eagles soaring overhead, and bears foraging along the shores, makes Alaska a premier destination for wildlife enthusiasts. Each tour offers a chance to connect with nature in a way that is both exhilarating and educational, ensuring that travelers of all ages leave with lasting memories.

One standout experience for families is the guided wildlife watching tours available in Juneau and Skagway. These excursions often include small-boat trips that navigate the stunning fjords, where you can spot humpback whales and sea lions. Local guides bring their expertise to the forefront, sharing insights about the animals' behaviors and the ecological importance of the regions you explore. Families can engage in hands-on experiences, such as learning about marine life during tidepool exploration, making the journey as much about education as it is about adventure.

Couples seeking a romantic escape will find that Alaska's wildlife tours can also offer intimate and serene experiences. Consider a sunset kayaking trip in Glacier Bay National Park, where you paddle alongside towering glaciers and observe seals lounging on ice fl oes. The tranquil setting, accompanied by the sounds of nature, provides an idyllic atmosphere for connection and reflection. Many operators provide gourmet picnics or wine pairings to enhance this romantic journey, making it a memorable highlight of your cruise.

For those interested in luxury accommodations, some wildlife tours offer premium experiences, such as private yacht charters that provide personalized service and exclusive viewing opportunities. Travelers can indulge in gourmet dining while cruising past breathtaking landscapes, ensuring that every moment is both lavish and comfortable. Operators like Alaskan Dream Cruises and UnCruise Adventures cater to this market, providing bespoke itineraries that allow for wildlife sightings and cultural immersion tailored to your preferences.

Finally, for those on a budget, Alaska's wildlife tours are accessible without sacrificing quality. Local operators often provide affordable group tours that allow you to experience the thrill of wildlife viewing without breaking the bank. Options such as the Glacier Wildlife Cruise in Seward or the Kenai Fjords National Park tours offer exceptional value, allowing you to witness the beauty of Alaska's wildlife at a fraction of the cost. Booking is straightforward; simply contact the tour providers directly at their listed numbers for reservations. With a range of options suited for every type of traveler, your Alaskan adventure awaits, promising unique experiences that will resonate long after your cruise ends.

Family-Friendly Activities

Alaska cruises offer an array of family-friendly activities that cater to various age groups and interests. From engaging wildlife encounters to exciting outdoor adventures, families can create lasting memories while exploring the breathtaking landscapes of the Last Frontier. One of the most popular activities is wildlife viewing, where families can spot majestic creatures such as whales, sea otters, and bald eagles. Many cruise lines provide guided excursions that enhance the experience, allowing families to learn more about the animals in their natural habitats. For a hands-on experience, consider booking a family-friendly wildlife cruise that includes educational programs tailored for children.

Another fantastic option for families is the chance to explore Alaska's stunning national parks, such as Glacier Bay and Denali. These parks offer a range of activities, including hiking, kayaking, and ranger-led programs that are designed to engage children and adults alike. Many cruise itineraries include stops at these parks, providing families with the opportunity to embark on unforgettable adventures. Don't forget to pack a picnic to enjoy amidst the breathtaking scenery, as it adds an extra layer of fun to your family outing.

For families seeking a more relaxed pace, many Alaska cruises feature onboard activities that cater to all ages. Kids' clubs and family-friendly entertainment options ensure that younger travelers are well entertained while adults can unwind. Options may include arts and crafts workshops, educational programs about Alaska's culture and history, and movie nights featuring films set in the region. Parents can take advantage of these activities to enjoy some time to themselves, knowing their children are engaged in safe and enjoyable pursuits.

Dining on an Alaska cruise can be a delightful experience for families, with many cruise lines offering diverse menus that cater to younger palates. Look for restaurants that provide children's menus or special dining experiences, such as themed dinners or interactive cooking classes. Additionally, some cruise lines feature family-friendly dining options where everyone can enjoy meals together in a relaxed atmosphere. Make sure to check for any dining packages that offer f l exibility, allowing you to plan your evenings around family activities.

Lastly, consider participating in shore excursions specifically designed for families. These excursions often include fun-filled activities such as dog sledding, zip-lining, or even visiting local farms and learning about sustainable practices. Companies like Alaska Shore Tours and Harv and Marv's offer family-friendly options that ensure everyone can participate and enjoy the unique experiences Alaska has to offer. When booking, don't hesitate to reach out to customer service representatives who can help you customize your itinerary to t your family's needs, ensuring an unforgettable adventure in this remarkable state.

Map of Beaches in Alaska

https://maps.app.goo.gl/HwJ8WxXhfefuYww8A

Chapter 6: Wildlife Encounters

Key Wildlife Species to Expect

When embarking on an Alaska cruise, travelers can anticipate encountering a rich tapestry of wildlife that is unique to the region. The majestic humpback whale is one of the most sought-after species, known for its acrobatic breaches and melodious songs that resonate through the icy waters. These magnificent creatures can often be spotted during the summer months as they migrate to the nutrient-rich waters of Alaska to feed. Whale-watching excursions are a popular activity, providing an unforgettable experience for families and couples alike, as knowledgeable guides share insights into these incredible mammals.

Another iconic species to expect is the bald eagle, a symbol of American wildlife. These birds, with their striking white heads and impressive wingspans, can frequently be seen soaring above coastal waters or perched majestically on tree branches. Observing a bald eagle in its natural habitat is a highlight for many cruise passengers, especially during excursions to places like the Chilkat Bald Eagle Preserve. Photography enthusiasts will find ample opportunities to capture the beauty of these birds as they hunt for f i sh or care for their young.

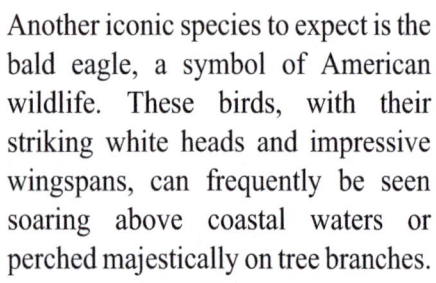

For those intrigued by terrestrial wildlife, the Alaskan brown bear is a must-see. These powerful animals are often spotted along streams and rivers, particularly during the salmon spawning season. Locations such as Katmai National Park offer guided bear viewing tours, allowing travelers to witness these magnificent creatures up close while ensuring safety and respect for their natural behavior. Families and couples can enjoy a thrilling adventure observing bears in their natural environment, making it a memorable part of their cruise experience.

Marine life is not limited to whales and eagles; the waters surrounding Alaska are also home to playful sea otters and sleek sea lions. Sea otters can often be seen f l oating on their backs, using stones to crack open shell fish, while sea lions are known for their loud barking and social behavior. Excursions that focus on marine wildlife provide the chance to learn more about these fascinating species and their roles in the ecosystem. This interaction with wildlife offers a unique perspective on the interconnectedness of life in Alaska's coastal regions.

Lastly, the diverse array of bird species, including puffins and seabirds, adds to the allure of an Alaskan cruise. Birdwatching enthusiasts will find joy in spotting these colorful and unique birds along the cliffs and shorelines. Many cruises include educational talks about the various species and their habitats, enhancing the overall experience for passengers. With so much wildlife to observe and appreciate, travelers can enrich their Alaska cruise adventure, creating lasting memories that resonate long after the journey concludes.

Responsible Wildlife Viewing Practices

Responsible wildlife viewing practices are essential for ensuring the preservation of Alaska's natural beauty and its diverse ecosystems. As you embark on your journey through Alaska's stunning landscapes, it is crucial to understand how your actions can impact the wildlife you encounter. Observing animals in their natural habitat can be a thrilling experience, but maintaining a respectful distance is vital. This not only protects the animals but also enhances your viewing experience, allowing you to appreciate their behavior without causing stress or disruption.

When approaching wildlife, always prioritize safety—for both yourself and the animals. Keep a minimum distance of at least 100 yards from large mammals such as bears and moose, and at least 50 yards from smaller animals like deer and wolves. Use binoculars or a camera with a zoom lens to observe them from afar. This practice minimizes the risk of startling the animals and allows you to watch their natural behaviors without interference. Remember, getting too close can provoke defensive reactions, leading to dangerous situations for both you and the wildlife.

Stay informed about the specific wildlife regulations in the areas you visit. Many sanctuaries and national parks have established guidelines designed to protect both the animals and their habitats. These regulations may include restrictions on the use of drones, which can disturb wildlife, and rules about feeding animals, which can lead to dependency on human food and alter their natural behaviors. Familiarizing yourself with these rules ensures that you contribute positively to conservation efforts and helps maintain the integrity of these delicate ecosystems.

Consider joining guided wildlife tours led by experienced naturalists. These professionals are trained to provide insights into animal behavior while emphasizing ethical viewing practices. They can help you navigate the best spots for wildlife sightings without disturbing natural habitats. Moreover, guided tours often support local conservation initiatives, allowing your adventure to contribute to the protection of the very wildlife you are there to enjoy. This way, you can engage in responsible viewing while enhancing your understanding of Alaska's unique fauna.

Lastly, educate yourself and your fellow travelers about the importance of wildlife conservation. Share your experiences and knowledge about responsible viewing practices with others on your cruise. Whether you are traveling as a family, a couple, or as part of a larger group, fostering a culture of respect for wildlife can amplify the positive impact of your adventure. By practicing and promoting responsible wildlife viewing, you not only improve your own experience but also play a significant role in protecting Alaska's incredible natural heritage for future generations.

Best Locations for Wildlife Spotting

Alaska is renowned for its breathtaking landscapes and diverse wildlife, making it a prime destination for those eager to experience nature at its nest. The Inside Passage offers numerous opportunities for wildlife spotting, particularly in areas such as Glacier Bay National Park. This UNESCO World Heritage site is home to an array of species, including humpback whales, sea lions, and puffins. Visitors can take advantage of guided boat tours that navigate the fjords, providing ample chances to observe these magnificent creatures in their natural habitat. For bookings, consider reaching out to local operators like Allen Marine Tours at 1-800-320-1202.

Another exceptional location is Kenai Fjords National Park, located near Seward. This park is famous for its glacial landscapes and rich marine life. Kayaking tours are a popular choice here, allowing adventurers to get up close with otters, seals, and even orcas. Many guided tours also include wildlife viewing as part of the experience, ensuring that guests maximize their chances of encountering Alaska's stunning fauna. For reservations, callers can contact Kenai Fjords Tours at 1-888-478-3346.

The coastal town of Sitka is also a hidden gem for wildlife enthusiasts. Known for its rich history and vibrant arts scene, Sitka also boasts remarkable wildlife viewing opportunities. The nearby Sitka National Historical Park and the waters surrounding it are ideal for spotting black bears, sea otters, and a variety of seabirds. Local fishing charters and eco-tours, such as those offered by Sitka Sound Tours, can be booked at 1-800-657-4546, providing unforgettable experiences for families and couples alike.

If you're venturing further north, Denali National Park is a must-visit for wildlife spotting. This iconic park is home to North America's highest peak and a myriad of wildlife, including grizzly bears, moose, and caribou. The park's shuttle buses offer guided tours that allow visitors to enjoy the stunning scenery while keeping an eye out for wildlife. For more information and bookings, contact the Denali Park Visitor Center at 1-800-622-7275.

Finally, no wildlife spotting adventure in Alaska would be complete without a visit to Kodiak Island. Known for its large population of Kodiak bears, the island provides unique opportunities for bear viewing, especially during the salmon spawning season. Various guided tours and lodges, such as Kodiak Island Adventures, can assist with arrangements for bear viewing excursions, reachable at 1-800-123-4567. This diverse range of locations ensures that every visitor can find their perfect wildlife experience while cruising through Alaska's stunning landscapes.

Chapter 7: Post-Cruise Options

Exploring Alaska After Your Cruise

Exploring Alaska after your cruise opens up a world of adventure and breathtaking beauty that extends far beyond the ship's dock. As you disembark from your cruise, the vast landscapes of Alaska invite you to experience its stunning natural wonders, rich culture, and vibrant cities. Whether you're a family seeking excitement, a couple looking for romance, or an individual interested in luxurious or affordable accommodations, Alaska has something to offer everyone. The key to maximizing your post-cruise experience lies in planning ahead to ensure you make the most of your time and budget.

For families, Alaska boasts numerous family-friendly activities that cater to all ages. From wildlife encounters to engaging museums, options abound. Consider visiting the Alaska SeaLife Center in Seward, where you can observe sea lions, otters, and a variety of marine life up close. Families can also enjoy guided tours through Denali National Park, offering opportunities to spot wildlife such as grizzly bears and moose. Booking a family-friendly tour in advance can enhance your experience, and local operators like Alaska Tour & Travel (1-800-208-0200) offer tailored packages for families.

Couples seeking a romantic getaway will find that Alaska's stunning scenery provides an idyllic backdrop for unforgettable moments. A scenic train ride on the Alaska Railroad offers breathtaking views of glaciers and mountains, perfect for a cozy outing. For a touch of luxury, consider booking a private dinner cruise in Juneau, where you can savor fresh seafood while watching the sunset over the water. Companies like Gastineau Guiding (1-877-789-5261) specialize in intimate experiences that cater to couples, allowing for a memorable evening that celebrates your time together.

When it comes to dining, Alaska features a diverse range of restaurants that showcase the region's culinary delights. For those craving fresh seafood, Tracy's King Crab Shack in Juneau is a must-visit, famed for its delicious crab dishes. For a more upscale dining experience, the Crow's Nest in Anchorage offers fine dining with stunning views, featuring locally sourced ingredients. Reservations are recommended, especially during peak seasons, and you can reach Crow's Nest at 1-800-276-7234. Exploring local eateries not only enhances your culinary experience but also provides insight into Alaska's unique culture.

Lastly, accommodations in Alaska range from luxurious hotels to budget-friendly lodges, catering to various preferences and budgets. The Hotel Alyeska in Girdwood provides a luxurious experience with stunning mountain views and spa services, while the Anchorage Downtown Hotel offers affordability without compromising comfort. Booking in advance is advisable, especially during the busy summer months. Websites like Booking.com can help you find the best deals, or you can call local hotels directly for special offers. With thoughtful planning and a sense of adventure, your post-cruise exploration of Alaska can be a remarkable journey filled with unforgettable experiences.

Recommended Tours and Activities

Alaska's breathtaking landscapes and unique wildlife create the perfect backdrop for a myriad of unforgettable tours and activities. For those embarking on a cruise in 2025 or 2026, a variety of excursions are available to suit different interests and budgets. One of the most popular options is a glacier viewing tour, where guests can witness the awe-inspiring sights of massive ice formations calving into the sea.
Companies like Allen Marine Tours

offer half-day excursions departing from Juneau, with booking available at 1-800-325-0146. This experience is ideal for families and couples alike, providing an opportunity to connect with nature while enjoying the stunning scenery.

For those seeking a more adventurous experience, consider a guided hiking tour through one of Alaska's majestic national parks. Denali National Park and Preserve, renowned for its wildlife and stunning vistas, offers various trails for all skill levels. Tour operators such as Alaska Wild Guides can arrange day hikes or multi-day excursions, with contact available at 1-907-783-2800. These tours not only provide physical activity but also the chance to encounter local wildlife, including moose, bears, and a plethora of bird species. This is an excellent way for families to bond while appreciating Alaska's natural beauty.

Cultural experiences are another highlight of Alaska's offerings. A visit to the Alaska Native Heritage Center in Anchorage provides insight into the rich history and traditions of Alaska's indigenous peoples. Guided tours are available, and reservations can be made by calling 1-907-330-8000. This activity is particularly enriching for families and couples interested in understanding the local culture, making it a memorable addition to any cruise itinerary. Engaging with local artisans and participating in workshops can enhance the understanding and appreciation of Alaska's diverse cultural heritage.

For those looking to indulge in luxury, a scenic seaplane tour over the stunning landscapes of the Inside Passage is highly recommended. Companies like Wings Airways offer breathtaking flights that showcase the beauty of glaciers and secluded fjords. Reservations can be made by calling 1-800-764-2293. This experience allows couples to enjoy a romantic adventure while taking in the majestic views from above. The combination of luxury and unparalleled scenery makes this tour a standout choice for those wanting to elevate their cruise experience.

Dining is an essential part of any trip, and Alaska boasts some remarkable culinary experiences. For top- notch seafood, The Crab Shack in Ketchikan is a must-visit, known for its fresh Dungeness crab and breathtaking waterfront views. Reservations can be made by calling 1-907-225-2025. For a more upscale dining experience, the Crow's Nest in Anchorage offers ne dining with an emphasis on local ingredients, and bookings can be secured at 1-907-276-0600. Checking out these recommended dining spots can enhance the cruising experience, allowing travelers to savor the unique f l avors of Alaska while enjoying the region's natural beauty.

Travel Tips for Extended Stays

When planning an extended stay in Alaska, whether as part of a cruise or a land excursion, it is essential to approach travel with a well-thought-out strategy. Prioritize f l exibility in your itinerary to allow for spontaneous adventures. The Alaskan wilderness is vast and unpredictable, and having a loose schedule can enable you to take advantage of opportunities that arise, such as wildlife sightings or last-minute excursions. Be prepared for varying weather conditions by packing layers and waterproof gear, ensuring that you can comfortably explore regardless of the elements.

Accommodation plays a crucial role in the overall experience of your trip. Depending on your budget and preferences, Alaska offers a range of options from luxurious lodges to affordable motels. Consider booking accommodations that provide amenities such as guided tours or transportation services, as these can enhance your stay. For luxury options, the Alyeska Resort in Girdwood and the Hotel Captain Cook in Anchorage are highly recommended. For budget-friendly stays, the Anchorage Downtown Hotel and Totem Inn in Seward offer comfortable lodging without breaking the bank. Always check for seasonal deals or packages that may provide additional value during your visit.

Dining experiences in Alaska are as diverse as the landscape itself. When exploring the culinary scene, be sure to sample local seafood, including halibut, salmon, and crab. Renowned restaurants such as Simon & Seafort's in Anchorage and The Crab Shack in Seward offer fresh, delicious options that showcase the region's bounty. For a unique experience, consider dining at the Girdwood Brewing Company, which pairs craft beers with tasty pub fare. Reservations are recommended during peak seasons, so planning ahead can help secure a table at these popular spots.

Transportation is another vital consideration for extended stays. While many cruise passengers may have access to onboard excursions, venturing out on your own can lead to unforgettable discoveries. Renting a car provides the freedom to explore at your own pace, especially in areas like the Kenai Peninsula or the Matanuska-Susitna Valley. Alternatively, utilizing the Alaska Railroad can offer scenic routes and a relaxing travel experience. For those who prefer guided experiences, local tour companies can arrange everything from day trips to multi-day excursions tailored to your interests.

Lastly, always stay informed about local events and festivals that may coincide with your visit. Alaska hosts a variety of celebrations that highlight its rich culture and traditions. Participating in these events can provide deeper insights into Alaskan life and create memorable experiences. Resources such as local tourism websites or visitor centers can be invaluable in discovering what's happening during your stay. Having a plan in place while remaining open to new experiences will ensure that your extended stay in Alaska is both enjoyable and fulfilling.

Map of Hiking Trails in Alaska

https://maps.app.goo.gl/eW6wAcxZMnxMjMjE8

Chapter 8: Booking Your Cruise

How to Book Your Alaska Cruise

Booking an Alaska cruise is a pivotal step in crafting an unforgettable adventure. Start by determining your travel dates and the duration of your cruise, as this will influence your itinerary and available options. The Alaska cruise season typically runs from late April to mid-September, with peak months being June to August. Research various cruise lines that operate in Alaska, including popular choices like Princess Cruises, Holland America Line, and Norwegian Cruise Line. Each offers unique experiences, amenities, and shore excursions, so understanding what each line provides will help you make an informed decision.

Once you have selected a cruise line, explore the specific itineraries they offer. Most cruises will include breathtaking ports such as Juneau, Ketchikan, and Skagway, as well as scenic cruising through Glacier Bay National Park or the Inside Passage. Take note of the different types of cabins available, from budget-friendly options to luxurious suites. Many cruise lines provide virtual tours of their ships and accommodations, allowing you to choose the perfect setting for your trip. For families, consider options with family suites or connecting cabins, while couples might enjoy romantic balcony rooms with stunning views.

Pricing can vary significantly based on your chosen cruise line, cabin type, and timing of booking. To maximize savings, consider booking early, as many cruise lines offer early-bird discounts or promotional deals. Alternatively, last-minute deals can yield substantial savings, though availability may be limited.

When calculating the total cost, remember to factor in additional expenses such as shore excursions, specialty dining, and onboard gratuities. Websites like Cruise Critic and Vacations To Go provide valuable insights and comparisons, ensuring you find the best deal that aligns with your budget.

When you're ready to book, you can do so through the cruise line's website, a travel agent, or a cruise-specific booking platform. If you prefer personalized service, a travel agent with expertise in Alaska cruises can help tailor your trip to meet your preferences. For direct bookings, contact the cruise line's customer service for assistance. Key phone numbers to keep handy are Princess Cruises at 1-800-774-6237, Holland America Line at 1-877-932-4259, and Norwegian Cruise Line at 1-866-234-7350. Don't hesitate to ask questions about the itinerary, onboard activities, and shore excursions during your booking process.

Finally, once your cruise is booked, start planning your onboard and shore experiences. Research the top dining options available on the cruise ship as well as renowned restaurants at each port of call. In Juneau, for instance, the Tracy's King Crab Shack is famous for its fresh seafood, while Ketchikan boasts the Alaska Fish House for local delicacies. Additionally, consider booking excursions in advance to secure your spots for popular activities like whale watching, glacier hiking, or wildlife tours. With a little preparation and research, your Alaska cruise adventure will be set for a remarkable exploration of this stunning destination.

Contact Information for Major Cruise Lines

When planning your Alaskan cruise adventure, having the right contact information for major cruise lines is essential for seamless booking and inquiries. This section provides a consolidated list of the leading cruise lines that operate in Alaska, along with their booking phone contacts, ensuring that you can easily reach out to them for any questions or reservations. Whether you are a family seeking a memorable vacation, a couple looking for a romantic getaway, or a traveler interested in luxury or affordable accommodations, this information will help you navigate your options effectively.

Princess Cruises is a popular choice for those exploring Alaska, known for its exceptional service and a wide range of itineraries. Travelers can reach Princess Cruises at 1-800-774-6237. With numerous family- friendly activities, onboard dining options, and excursions tailored to showcase the stunning Alaskan wildlife, Princess Cruises is well-suited for various vacationers. Their itineraries often include visits to Glacier Bay National Park and the charming towns of Skagway and Juneau.

Holland America Line offers a blend of luxury and adventure, making it a favored option for couples and those seeking a more upscale experience. For bookings and inquiries, you can contact Holland America Line at 1-877-932-4259. Their ships feature award-winning dining and exclusive shore excursions that highlight the natural beauty and rich culture of Alaska. With a focus on exploration, Holland America provides opportunities for wildlife viewing and cultural enrichment, ensuring an unforgettable journey.

Norwegian Cruise Line is another excellent choice, appealing to travelers who desire flexibility and a relaxed atmosphere. Their contact number for bookings is 1-888-625-2784. Known for their "freestyle cruising" concept, Norwegian allows guests to dine at their convenience and enjoy a variety of entertainment options. Families will appreciate the diverse activities available onboard, making it an ideal choice for those traveling with children and looking for an engaging vacation experience.

Finally, for those on a tighter budget yet seeking an enriching Alaskan experience, Carnival Cruise Line is a commendable option. You can book your cruise by calling 1-800-764-7419. Carnival is known for its fun, vibrant atmosphere and affordability, making it suitable for families and first-time cruisers. With a variety of itineraries that include stops at stunning Alaskan ports, Carnival provides an excellent introduction to the wonders of Alaska without compromising on the quality of service and experience.

By utilizing this contact information for major cruise lines, you can make informed decisions about your Alaskan cruise adventure. Whether you prioritize luxury, affordability, or family-oriented experiences, each cruise line offers unique features tailored to enhance your travel experience. Be sure to call ahead for the latest deals and to secure your spot on a remarkable journey through the breathtaking landscapes of Alaska.

Tips for Getting the Best Deals

When planning an Alaska cruise, securing the best deals is crucial for enhancing your overall experience without straining your budget. One of the most effective strategies is to book early. Cruise lines often offer significant discounts for those who reserve their spots months in advance. This is particularly beneficial for families or couples looking for specific cabin types or amenities, as popular options can fill up quickly. Additionally, keep an eye out for promotional offers during travel expos or cruise line events, where exclusive deals may be available.

Another effective tip is to remain flexible with your travel dates. If your schedule allows, consider cruising during the shoulder season, which typically includes late April to early June or September. These times often boast lower prices while still providing a wonderful experience with fewer crowds. Additionally, weekday departures may also come with reduced fares compared to weekend sailings. Use fare comparison websites to track price fluctuations and identify the best time to book your desired itinerary.

Utilizing loyalty programs can also yield substantial savings. Many cruise lines offer rewards for repeat customers, including discounts, onboard credits, or complimentary upgrades. If you are a frequent cruiser, or if you intend to become one, signing up for these programs can lead to long-term benefits. Furthermore, consider booking your cruise through a travel agent who specializes in cruises. They often have access to exclusive deals and packages that are not available to the general public, which can enhance your experience while minimizing costs.

Exploring package deals is another avenue worth pursuing. Many cruise lines offer bundled options that include accommodations, excursions, and onboard credits. This not only simplifies planning but can also lead to significant savings. Look for packages that align with your interests, whether you're seeking luxury experiences or family-friendly activities. It's essential to read the ne print to ensure that the included amenities meet your expectations and needs, ensuring a smooth experience.

Lastly, dining on your cruise can also impact your budget. While many cruise lines offer an array of dining options, consider balancing your meals between complimentary restaurants and specialty dining venues. This strategy allows you to enjoy gourmet meals without overspending. Research the top restaurants on your cruise line and make reservations as soon as possible, as popular spots will ll quickly. Additionally, inquire about any dining packages that may provide discounts on multiple specialty meals, ensuring you savor the best culinary experiences Alaska has to offer without breaking the bank.

Chapter 9: Conclusion

Recap of Key Points

In the exploration of Alaska's breathtaking landscapes and vibrant culture, it is essential to **recap** the key points that will enhance your cruise experience in 2025/2026. First and foremost, understanding the various cruise options available is crucial. Families, couples, and solo travelers alike can choose from luxury liners that offer world-class amenities to more affordable options that do not compromise on experience. Each cruise line presents unique itineraries, making it important to select one that aligns with your interests, whether it be wildlife viewing, cultural experiences, or breathtaking scenery.

Another vital aspect of planning your Alaskan adventure is securing accommodations that cater to your specific needs. This guide emphasizes a range of lodging options, from luxurious hotels with stunning views to budget-friendly motels that provide comfort without breaking the bank. Additionally, booking contacts are provided to simplify the reservation process, ensuring that your stay complements your cruise experience seamlessly. Prioritizing accommodation will allow you to focus on enjoying the myriad of activities Alaska has to offer.

Dining plays a significant role in any travel experience, and Alaska is no exception. The recap of top restaurants highlights dining establishments that reflect the local culture and cuisine, offering everything from fresh seafood to traditional Alaskan dishes. Families will appreciate kid-friendly menus, while couples can enjoy romantic settings with gourmet meals. Knowing where to dine will enhance your cruising experience, as meals become an integral part of enjoying Alaska's unique f l avors.

Wildlife is undoubtedly one of Alaska's main attractions, and understanding the best times and locations to witness these magnificent a cent creatures is essential. This guide provides insights into the most effective ways to spot whales, bears, and other wildlife, ensuring that your cruise is filled with unforgettable moments. Whether you are embarking on excursions or enjoying wildlife from the comfort of your ship, maximizing these experiences will enrich your overall journey.

Lastly, the importance of planning and preparation cannot be overstated. The logistics of booking your cruise, arranging accommodations, and selecting dining options can seem overwhelming, but this guide aims to simplify the process. By focusing on key points and providing essential contacts, it enables travelers to make informed decisions without sifting through excessive information. Embrace the adventure that awaits in Alaska, and let the memories you create on this remarkable journey be the highlight of your travel experiences.

Final Tips for an Unforgettable Alaska Cruise

When planning an unforgettable Alaska cruise, it's essential to prioritize your itinerary and choose the right ports of call. Each Alaskan destination offers unique experiences, from the breathtaking glaciers of Juneau to the vibrant culture of Ketchikan. Researching each port's attractions will allow you to create a tailored experience that aligns with your interests, whether you're traveling as a couple, with family, or seeking luxury or affordability. Consider booking excursions in advance, as popular activities can fill up quickly, ensuring you don't miss out on must-see sights.

Accommodations play a crucial role in maximizing your cruise experience. While many cruise lines offer a variety of cabin options, it can be beneficial to look into pre- and post-cruise stays in Alaska. For those seeking luxury, consider properties like the Hotel Alyeska in Girdwood, renowned for its stunning mountain views and exceptional amenities. For families or budget-conscious travelers, options like the Anchorage Grand Hotel provide comfortable stays without breaking the bank. Make sure to book early and check for any special promotions that might enhance your stay.

Dining is an integral part of your cruise experience, and Alaska boasts a rich culinary scene. Research the top restaurants in each port you plan to visit, such as Tracy's King Crab Shack in Juneau, where you can savor the freshest seafood. For a fine dining experience, consider the Glacier Bay Lodge, which offers exquisite local dishes with stunning views of the surrounding landscape. Many cruise lines also feature onboard dining experiences that highlight Alaskan cuisine; be sure to make reservations for any specialty restaurants to secure your spot.

Wildlife watching is one of the prime attractions during an Alaskan cruise. To enhance your chances of spotting iconic wildlife, such as whales, bears, and eagles, consider scheduling excursions led by experienced naturalists. These guided tours not only provide insight into the animals' habitats but also ensure a more eco-friendly experience. Keep your camera ready and be patient; the rewards of witnessing these majestic creatures in their natural environment are well worth the wait.

Lastly, staying connected with fellow travelers and sharing experiences can enrich your journey. Engage with online communities or social media groups focused on Alaska cruises, where you can exchange tips, recommendations, and personal stories. Don't hesitate to reach out to your cruise line's customer service for any questions or concerns leading up to your trip. For booking inquiries, you can contact major cruise lines such as Princess Cruises at 1-800-774-6237 or Holland America Line at 1-800-426-0327. With careful planning and a spirit of adventure, your Alaskan cruise will undoubtedly be a memorable experience.

BONUS
TRAVEL PLANNER

7 DAY TRIP

Travel Planner

Day 1 : Destination - _____

Activities:
_____
_____
_____

Day 2 : Destination - _____

Activities:
_____
_____
_____

Day 3 : Destination - _____

Activities:
_____
_____
_____

Day 4 : Destination - _____

Activities:
_____
_____
_____

7 DAY TRIP
Travel Planner

Day 5 : Destination - _____
Activities:
_____
_____
_____

Day 6 : Destination - _____
Activities:
_____
_____
_____

Day 7 : Destination - _____
Activities:
_____
_____
_____

Final Note:
_____
_____
_____
_____

TRAVEL BUDGET PLANNER

Travel Budget

Date: _____
Destination: _____

Transportation

Item	Estimated Cost	Actual Cost
	$	$
	$	$
	$	$
	$	$
	$	$

Accommodation

Item	Estimated Cost	Actual Cost
	$	$
	$	$
	$	$
	$	$
	$	$

Food & Dining

Item	Estimated Cost	Actual Cost
	$	$
	$	$
	$	$
	$	$
	$	$

Activities & Tours

Item	Estimated Cost	Actual Cost
	$	$
	$	$
	$	$
	$	$
	$	$

Local Transport

Item	Estimated Cost	Actual Cost
	$	$
	$	$
	$	$
	$	$
	$	$

Shopping & Souvenirs

Item	Estimated Cost	Actual Cost
	$	$
	$	$
	$	$
	$	$
	$	$

Notes

NOTEPAD

date   /   NOTES

date /   NOTES

Printed in Dunstable, United Kingdom

BLACK SUGAR

a book of poetry

and innermost thoughts.

By Zakiya Raines

COPYRIGHT

All rights reserved, including the right to reproduce this book or portions thereof in any form whatsoever. For information, address the publisher. Cover Art by Zakiya Raines.

All rights reserved. This book or parts thereof may not be reproduced in any form, stored in any retrieval system, or transmitted in any form by any means—electronic, mechanical, photocopy, recording, or otherwise—without prior written permission of the publisher, and author, except as provided by United States of America copyright law. For permission requests, write to the publisher, or author at "Attention: Permissions Coordinator," at the address below: www.zakiyaraines.com.

©2021 Zakiya Raines

Dream Realm

After I closed my eyes

I flew to a place

It was a hotel

It was a museum

In the middle of the ocean

On 5th avenue

The sidewalks were made of rare jewels and

diamonds

I went to a gala

Everyone was there.

I danced in a white dress

My body was beautiful

I was alone and blissful

I woke up

Then fell back to reality

I opened my eyes to the sunrise,

And I bumped my head on the truth.

The pain made me lay back down,

With tears in my eyes,

I drifted off back to sleep

I flew

Just to be with you

Again.

On my back

Lying on my back,

Watching a star.

I think of you

Videos before bed

I can't sleep

I creep into my secret drawer

My hands creep past my navel

You are all I can think of

Bursts of fantasy tremor through my avatar

Unfortunately

I am starving

simply imagining steak will never be enough

to satiate me.

I must have you.

Play

Trousers slumped on the floor.

My boots are still zipped.

Undressed yourself like a tornado.

Wait.

I want to see a show.

Broadway is closed.

But it's open tonight.

Peepshows shutdown in Times Square.

Give me a peep

Here in your living room.

Show

Me how you like it

When you are alone

Show

Me what you want.

Play

Perform for me.

Stroke.

Show

Me what I am getting into.

I like monologues.

I love to sit in the front row

Of an empty theatre.

I'm in the mood for a salacious soliloquy.

What a monumental

microphone you have.

A bank doesn't invest resources where there will not be a return. And neither should you. Money, time, energy, physicality, and love are resources.

People tend to take for granted and place a low

value upon that which they did not have to work

for,

or sacrifice for.

That includes love.

Fine Lines

You cross my boundaries.

What was once a bold, black line,

Has now been whittled to a thin fine line.

I look at the fine lines on your face.

So many fine lines,

You should have so much wisdom.

What good is age without wisdom?

What good is love without care?

The small lines are blurred

Fantasy and reality

Sanity and insanity

I am so sane

I am so sober

Or maybe I have already lost it

Maybe everything around me is just a dream.

Nothing is as it used to seem.

Mother

Because

I would work my hands raw to give to you

I have worn my body down to feed you

I have spilled my blood repeatedly

so you could enter this earth.

I would do anything for you

I would use my bare hands to end another.

I would enter the most dangerous den

to save you.

My loyalty will remain unbroken

Even when I leave this earth,

I will still love you.

When I pass into the next realm,

I will still fight for you

I will speak to angels and rally on your behalf.

I always want what is best for you.

I will hold your hand in times of weakness.

I will hold you.

Counsel you in times of strength.

You will know what love is.

I love you unconditionally I give my all to you.

I believe in you.

Everything that I will leave on this earth,

I prepare to leave for you

I will never give up on you

Because I am your mother.

Beach day

The sun beams bright

I can feel the warmth on my skin

Grateful for these last warm days of fall.

I look at my children and think how they soon will

be

No longer small.

My days are so full

I feel empty

I need something to call my own

A legacy

An inner space where I feel bliss

Where only my thoughts exist

I need to get back to the space

Where my needs are being met

When I breathe in peace

I

Need

Me.

Lovers and givers must set limits, because takers and warlords have no limits and will leave you with nothing.

There are few things that can evoke the same level of dread as someone taking their mask off, and immediately realizing it's too late.

Doctors cut off bad limbs, to ward off rot and

infection.

Surely you can cut off bad people, to ward off rot

and destruction in your life,

no matter what the connection.

Reciprocity

I just search around each day

For you

I open my cabinets mindlessly

I look in my refrigerator

I watch the tv

But you are not there.

I am stuck here in this reality

Without you

Why is there so much pain in existence?

Did you even incarnate?

Did you decide to stay behind at the last moment?

Where are you?

Why must I spend my life with an empty android?

A poor replacement, a placeholder for you?

I want to love someone wildly and madly

And be loved the same

In return.

Why is reciprocity so much to ask for?

I am dying inside

Dying for something so basic

Each day I struggle to keep my spirit alive

I smile and well-wish

On the inside I am wailing.

Recognize you

I'll recognize you

By the way you feel when I speak to you

By your eyes

By your touch

By the uniqueness of your presence

By the way you will recognize me

I will stalk your dreams

Until I can have you in my arms

Have me

I watch you and I cannot touch you.

I just want to tell you that you can have me.

If you are sad and you need someone to make

you laugh, you can have me.

If you are sick and need someone to nurse you

back to health, you can have me.

If you are in need of holding and love,

you can have me.

If you are feeling down on yourself,

you can have me,

I will list all the ways that you are supreme.

If you need someone to sit in silence with,

You can have me.

When you need someone to love you,

You can have me.

You can have me,

Because I love you.

I already love you.

It is simple.

Have me.

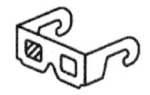

The wrong person will make you feel like what you want is always too much. The right person will make you feel like what you want is natural.

If you have to explain to someone repeatedly how to treat you right, they have zero desire to treat you right. Lace up those sneakers and run.

Don't spend your time worrying and stressing yourself out, over someone who can't ask you how your day was, and ACTUALLY listen to the answer.

No need for words

There is no need for words.

I know you.

I've seen your soul.

I know your face.

Fold yourself into my arms,

Taste my embrace.

I am a flavor that you already know.

Don't be shy,

Fill yourself on my vibe.

Fill me up with our tribe.

My chalice has been waiting for you.

Only you can mend

That which has been broken.

Empty

You roll

Your body onto mine.

No fanfare.

You do the moves you've rehearsed.

I know your lines.

You can't care to deviate from the script.

I am tired of this movie

I've seen it thousands of times

It ends badly.

You empty yourself

Swiftly

Overzealously

Loudly proclaiming your perceived

accomplishment.

I need a new movie

I need a new script

I am empty.

Living without love is so gray.

When you need someone to be there, and they don't show up for you, remember that.

People will explain to you, without words, what you truly mean to them, if you just be quiet for a minute.

In love, no one wants to be second place.

Everyone wants to be someone's gold medal.

The hardest times often reveal the softest of hearts.

If they could see.

If they could see

How you talk to me

When no one is around.

Everyone thinks you're so sweet

They think you're so kind.

If they could see

The way you ambush me emotionally

With your words

Neglect me with your orchestrated silence.

If everyone could see

What kind of a man

You really

Be.

Troubled waters

There is a hole in our vessel.

We are in the open water.

Everyone thinks we are sailing in a shiny yacht.

It is a mirage.

I am drowning on your dinghy.

Every time I have the chance to save myself,

I turn back.

One day I will let go.

Let the tide

Take me back to shore.

If I were invisible, I could watch a gorgeous, striking man move for hours.

When you think of all the chemistry that needs to exist, in order for simple things to occur, there really is no such thing as simple.

Love will endure, but not through every and anything. True love will not force you to endure. If love is a test of endurance, then it surely isn't love.

Affection is mandatory, not optional. The same for reciprocity.

Sustenance.

When I am done feeding your belly
I want to feed your soul
I want to nurture your spirit
I want you to fill my belly
With the next generation
From our spiritual family.

Never good enough

You wanted a blue book.
I went and got you the blue book.
You weren't happy.
You wanted a yellow moon.
I found one for you and gave it to you.
I disrupted the tides and the shape of life in
another galaxy for you.
You still weren't happy.
You snuffed out the light in my spirit,
and you smiled.
My death made you happy.

Interior Design

On the 8th time we broke bread
You broke my headboard
And dented my sheetrock.
We debated about politics
Philosophy
Eastern beliefs
And parenting strategies.
You patched and fixed my walls.
Each Sunday thereafter
Became a routine.
Break bread,
Redecorate.
You had a rebuttal for everything,
Even me.
You bought me a new bed
But still broke my heart.
I will always miss
The way you rearranged my furniture.

I'm not sure if I love the idea of you,
or if I love how you make me feel.

Believe.

There can be no doubt
Only belief
Only faith
Only love
Only conviction
Only knowing
In this space
Is where God shows up
To help you perform miracles.

Eyes

I don't like the way you look at me.
Your eyes are angry
Menacing
A dark force within you.
You used to look at me with love.
Now I turn to catch you staring
Planning
With hidden contempt.

Don't allow the naysayers to break you down with their fears and bias, you are on earth with some particular work to do. It's your calling, not theirs.

If you find yourself constantly working to keep something, or hold on to it, perhaps you need to let it go. Even mother manages to let go each winter.

I spent many years carrying around so much baggage. When I finally stopped to take inventory, to see what was slowing me down, I saw that most of the baggage was not even mine. When I left all the baggage where I found it, and gave it back to its original owner, magical things started happening in my life.

No other feeling

I can't think of a feeling that can compare
To holding you in my arms.
The first time I looked at your face,
You made my spirit exponentially happy.
You smelled like new life.
My body taught me how to feed you
God gave me everything I needed to take care of you
There was a clap of thunder
As you were put into my womb
Your everything was formed within me.
As long as I live
Nothing will change the love I have for you.
I am so proud
Every time I hear your voice say
Mom

You cannot make someone respect you.
You can walk away from being disrespected.

If there is not one creator joining us all together, explain to me why a phallus+scrotum looks like a traditional key and a female orifice looks like a keyhole.

Need

I need
For you to love me
For you to act like it.
For you to be the missing piece
Of my mystery.
I need
You to reach places
No one else can.
I need for you to find
the hard-to-reach corners,
I need
For you to save the girl
That's drowning
Deep in the maze.
I would give you the key
If I could only trust you.

Naked

After everyone goes to bed
I dance to the slow music in my heart
I turn my speakers up loud
I close my eyes
I undress until my spirit is exposed,
Where no one can see.
I dance in tune with the spirits around me.
I leave my body and fly around the room.
I see myself and my bare skin is draped in gold baubles and stones from mother earth. My nipples point through the shiny necklaces and jewelry draped around my waist and hips. My ankles are covered in the elements of my ancestors. My hands clap and my wrists make music with the clang of the gems and elements of the motherland.

The spirits show themselves in the dark light of

the candles.

It is a reunion.

We drink together and laugh.

We are in a dark room,

Dancing by the candlelight.

"We know" they say.

Telling me "Everything is going to be okay".

When the music is over

They spread their wings

Kiss me on each cheek

And walk me to bed,

Sending me to my dreams

With messages,

By the quiet

Bright

Moonlight.

Remember that Love must match actions. Love is an action word.

Your inner dialogue predicts your outer experience.

Even if your parents were terrible, even if your siblings were monsters, it's never an excuse to just treat people badly. You are responsible for how you treat people each day.

Expect that any energy that you put into the universe will be returned. This means extremely high vibrations and not-so-high vibrations. Like honey, energy has no expiration date.

Exhumation

I am looking to transform

Back to the person I really am.

Who I was born to be,

before the many ways

I died.

I need to find the child

Murdered by life's circumstances

I am going to her grave

I am going to dig down to her

I will bring her back to life

Even if it kills

My new one.

I am through living a dead life

I am exhuming myself.

Exorcism

My head was drawn to yours like a magnet

As you walked into my orbit.

I knew immediately.

Voices whispered to me

All the female ancestors in my red chakra

Chanted in unison.

The countdown began immediately.

All I needed to do

was wait for you to come to me.

Right on time

Here you are floating to me.

I wonder if you know why you are here.

I am going to reach into your ethereal

You can claim your rightful place

You will sit on a throne I have made for you

Eat from a table that I have made with my own hands

You will drink love and kindness

After much libation

You will exorcise me

Of my worldly woes and wounds

Only you can make my head spin

Neck twisting

Back curved

Like roman architecture.

Dewed and shiny.

Whether you know it or not,

I know what you are.

I know who you're here for.

Swim

The feeling of the water on my skin
The water pushes me playfully
It is asking for me to join in
The water immediately wraps around my body
Softly holding me up towards the sun.
The fish come to greet me.
I want to swim with the orcas.
I want to swim with the whale sharks.
The sea stars
Blow me tiny kisses with their tube feet.
The water feels like a bath
I make my way back to the tiny white sand
Water kisses me
lays me back on the shore.
Until we meet again.

Don't insist on going out of your way for someone who insists on standing in your way.

The best blessing

I prayed for the pain to end

God blessed me

With indifference

The best blessing

Was falling out of love with you.

I don't need your love.

I don't need your love anymore.

If someone makes many promises and doesn't keep them, that person is poisonous to your spirit. Run.

Once the fairytale cannot be reclaimed, it's time to retreat and reassess.

Simply wanting someone is not enough.
Appreciating, valuing, and understanding them is the ultimate goal.

If a person doesn't listen to you when you speak, stop speaking to them.

Warden

I am not allowed to love

I am not allowed to speak

I am not permitted to have my own thoughts

I am not entitled to my own opinion

I do not have the right to my body.

You are not a lover

You are a warden.

Folded

I keep you hidden

Deep in my thoughts

I take you out when I need to feel happy

The birds sing

I think of you

A favorite song

comes on

I unfold you from the back of my mind

An instant living hologram.

Take me to our favorite place

In our fantastical space.

Jackhammer

What are the origins of your inseam?

I am trying to measure the rise

With my eyes

Unaided

I think I need to get closer

Examine the seat up close

To get a better idea

Of what kind of power

Is in your impact

Last name hammer

First name jack

People forget to account for ethereal diseases, as well as venereal. Ethereal can linger for lifetimes.

A person can say that they love you, but then treat you terribly. Understand that this isn't love, this is manipulation and gaslighting. Words must match actions.

In prompted life, a person can show you that they care, with their actions, because they know how to play the role and read the script. In real life, a person who loves you will do so, without being prompted, without being asked, simply because it is in their heart to do so. Real love is unscripted.

If you have to wonder if they love you, THEY DON'T.

Each day go out of your way to speak positivity and truth to someone who may need it. You never know how much your words may breathe life into a person who needs it.

Dance

Feeling your skin

Against mine

Notes floating on the balmy air

No clocks

Chest to chest

Cheek to cheek

Hip to hip

Your body has melded into mine

Just under the cobblestone arch

Feels like home

Dancing every night

With you.

Foreign Language

I was trapped in the forest

No one could understand me

I asked for directions

I said my name

All I received were confused looks

Mysterious sounds fell out of their faces

Eyes glazed over

Showing me their backs.

I roamed

Starving

Giving up hope with each interaction

One ounce left.

I saw you in the forest

You spoke to me

I opened my mouth to speak

Smiling

You said your name.

We speak the same language.

Bathe

Wanting

Wanton

Wriggling

Friction.

Writhing

Warning.

Withdraw rapidly.

Bring the baster to my lips.

Lip gloss like bodywash.

Bathe me.

Touch It

Sit across from me.

I wore a skirt today.

I have a dresser full of lacy things.

But

Couldn't seem to find the right ones for today.

My mama raised me to cross my legs.

I forget sometimes.

I wore the shoes you love so much.

I know you see

Do you want to feel?

I know you want to feel it.

Don't worry,

I'll feel it for you.

You look around to see

If anyone sees.

Keep drinking your coffee.

Don't be shy now.

It's no secret.

We both know

You sat there for one reason

And one reason only

To watch.

If we don't share the same intentions for each other,
we are just wasting each other's time.

I need to be pleased and pleasing,

in life, at this point.

I've had enough teasing.

Don't just say you love me.

Be love.

Do love,

So, I can believe love.

Sometimes the best thing you can do for love, is to show them the door.

Never ever regret being deserted by someone you loved. It is all part of the plan of the trash taking itself out. Don't make the mistake of trying to bring the hefty bag back into the house.

Never take responsibility for someone else's poor choice patterns. They did it before you, are doing it to you, and will continue doing it after you. Take responsibility for yourself and leave them where you found them. They don't need you; they need therapy.

Pieces of Trust

Every time

You hold me

I put a bit of my weight on you.

I know I can lose a little of my balance

Give a little of myself,

A piece of my trust.

I trust you.

I know you won't let me down.

You can't,

You're just not made that way.

The factory burned down

After they manufactured you.

I see traces of the cosmos

In your construction.

Mother earth was showing off

When she made you.

New York Sunset

Dark blue on orange

Balmy air.

Dining Al Fresco

Ella emanating into the streets

Nat King Cole serenading.

Candles flickering

Low lights make silhouettes in your eyes

Fireflies make Marquees

Around the leaves.

Pockets of warm air,

concupiscence populates the shadows.

Tasting lips behind fragrant flowering trees.

Birds doing the waltz.

Squirrels dance the salsa.

Bees do the Bomba

In your orbit

Butterflies tango in your halo.

The crickets croon

And the grasshoppers do the Aduma.

Unwrap me

Unfold me

In the Amphitheatre of the open air.

I am still hungry

Partaking in a hot sausage roll

Being turned into a pretzel.

No sauce on the side sir

Sauce all over

In fact, squirt a little extra sir.

Huge shoes

Mammoth man

Immense mess.

Call the front desk

The mattress needs to be redressed.

New linens

Free from stress

Sliding doors aside

Veranda open

Curtains fly like sails.

We fall into perfect slumber

Bodies still tingling

After a thorough and tailored wringing.

Everyone deserves to be loved the way they desire. Everyone deserves to give love, the way they define it. However, no one is obligated to accept love in a way that makes them feel unloved.

With the right person,

even silence is special.

Find a way to share your joy,

share your love,

with the people who savor,

and appreciate,

your acts of love and kindness.

Sharing experience and wisdom,

Is an act of love and kindness.

Being able to receive wisdom

is an act of love.

It takes a remarkable human being to recognize their own pain and not inflict that same pain onto others.

There is a difference between a person having a terrible day and having a terrible heart. The former you can get through, the latter you must free yourself from.

I'm not for everybody, and I am completely okay with that.

Angels

The little bits of glitter in the air

I inspect them closer

They speak to me

They tell me things

They tell me my future

They show me who I am

They show me what I am to do

Their love is purely internal

They tell me

not to be powered by the external.

I converse with them

I learn

I learn how to let go

How to let go with pleasure.

Love on Ice

The glow of the lights

The beat of the speakers

The energy of the night

I am walking through

The world is my playground

Crystal ball in my palm

Psychic's in my hips

Arrive to me

I am here to hydrate you

Mind, body, and spirit.

I've had my eye on you

You know

I have

Exactly

What you need.

Cyclone

Hoover was inspired by me,

Black and Decker took notes,

Dyson created suction after me,

Miele tried to win in the knees-down melee,

Shark attempted to copy my service,

Electrolux can't rival my dedication.

Kenmore won't compare

Emerson can't begin

to compete with my suction.

There are some people in life who think "I had to go through that (insert painful event here), so you should have to suffer through it as well."

There are others who feel "I had to go through that (insert painful event here), so I don't want anyone else to feel that intense pain."

Be the second person.

One of the most cruel and heartless things a person can do is pretend to believe in someone's dreams, never really wanting to be a part of them.

I sometimes wish that I when I met people, there was a special setting on my glasses, so I could see their insides, their intentions, and see their soul. I've wasted so much time on people who only *appeared* to have a soul,

and had nothing but bottomless darkness on the inside.

Pockets

You asked me to help you look for something.

Your hands are too big to fit in the silk suit pockets you say.

I am looking for something

I cannot find

I open your suit jacket

Breastpocket.

The other one is empty too.

Turn around

rear pockets.

Front pants pockets.

Endless deep pockets

Skin.

Lunchbox.

Warm corn on the cob.

I am trapped in your inseam.

You won't let go

Of my elbow.

I think you need a seamstress,

There's an arm-sized hole in this pocket.

Chrysalis

Close friends

Confidantes

Crossing the line.

I have ventured into an unknown realm

My now has been destroyed

rippling changes into my future

raising the standard

of human of possibility

Rewire my nerves

Illuminate my spirit

From the inside

With your flashlight.

Vibrate the place where my soul connects to my avatar

I am levitating

Beneath you.

I am wrinkled

wet

unfolded.

Legs shaking in chorus

My knees are wingtips

a newly emerged butterfly

From my chrysalis.

I had no idea that I was your caterpillar.

Printed in Great Britain
by Amazon